My *3*Year*s* of Living Peacefully

A dad's journey of trying to be a
nice guy

Mark Ellison

For my kids,
and their kids,
and their kids

CONTENTS

INTRODUCTION

In 2013 I started writing a book – *"You Are Infinite, You Are Eternal, You Are God: And more importantly You Are Me"*. But a year later I figured I didn't really have the cred to be taken seriously (particularly with a title like that). So I stopped writing and decided I needed to embody what I am actually talking about before I could finish it. It's one thing to believe on a cognitive level that every one of us is inextricably linked to each other and all that is (God), but another thing altogether to be able to consistently put that into practice in my daily life.

So at the start of 2014 I made it my primary goal in life to *be peace*. I wanted to *be* the love that I know forms the quantum strings of energy that are the One Interconnected All That Is – the Fabric of the Cosmos. Basically, I wanted to live as God – with unconditional peace and love at all times. As a teacher and senior school leader, with four kids under seven, and a wife with a really busy schedule as well, and as someone who tends to have a fairly short temper, this wasn't going to be easy. But having had some great mentors and inspiration in my life, I reckon I had a good base to give it a solid crack.

Before I knew it, my one year of living peacefully turned into three. Did I find nirvana? Did I become an enlightened master living in a state of constant bliss? No. Not even close! But I definitely got a lot better, and I learnt a lot along the way. Nine months in I started writing down some of my insights and reflections. These became my daily mantras and regular reminders of how to live the life I wanted to live. This book is a collection of these insights, mantras and reflections. Days when I remembered these ideas and practices, life was truly awesome. This experience, and these ideas have made me a much better husband, father, teacher, and person in general. By sharing them with you, I hope you might find some benefit too.

Love and peace.

1

YOU ARE INFINITE, YOU ARE ETERNAL, YOU ARE GOD!

AND MORE IMPORTANTLY, YOU ARE ME

Tuesday 30 September 2014

O.K - so I should probably explain what it is exactly that I have come to believe that I want to share with the world. So here is the introduction to my book that I wrote during the second half of 2013. Hope it makes sense...

'INTRODUCTION

"A human being is part of the whole, called by us 'universe'; a part limited in time and space. He experiences himself, his thoughts and feelings as something separated from the rest—a kind of optical delusion of his consciousness. This delusion is a kind of prison for us, restricting us to our personal desires and to affection for a few persons nearest us. Our task must be to free ourselves from this prison."

~ Albert Einstein

So what does it mean to say you are infinite, you are eternal, you are God?

You are infinite – you are everyplace and everywhere. There is nowhere in the unimaginable vastness of the cosmos (and beyond the cosmos) that you are not.

You are eternal – you have always been, and you always will be. You will never end.

You are God – if you have an idea in your head that God can either be proved or disproved – that it is even possible to debate the existence of God – then that idea is not God. God is simply the sum reality of all that is – whatever that is - and therefore the only reality. That reality is incontestable. That reality is you!

To many people of faith, this final statement will be highly offensive. It does not need to be. Each of the major faith traditions preach the divinity that exists within each human

2

being. The problem is that few people have ever taken it seriously. Far from threatening an individual's faith, realising the truth in the above statements can deeply strengthen and enhance their belief system and spirituality.

At your most fundamental level of awareness and being, you already know this. The conscious human mind has tricked you into believing otherwise – to believing you are a tiny, separate being, limited, as Einstein puts it, in time and space. As arguably the greatest mind in history, Einstein's greatest ever insight can be found in the quote above. Our task *must* be to free ourselves of the prison that is our illusion of being separate from the rest of creation. This book will help you rediscover the truth that you have always known.

Most importantly however, this book will give you the realisation that, as you are infinite, eternal, and God, then you are inextricably ME. You ARE every other person, and every creature on the planet. You are the planet! You are creation, you are life itself. The implications of this realisation are profound. "Knowing" this – actualising this realisation in "your" life – means you love all of creation as yourself. It means the end of hate, anger, violence – the end of war, famine and suffering. It is the foundation of true inner (and therefore outer) peace.

Are you ready to live this realisation?

Author's note: As a completely amateur writer, I claim to be an expert on zero of the fields that will be discussed in the following pages! There are dozens of experts, books, videos and studies that provide much greater detail on the absolute interconnectedness of all of creation. My purpose here is not to replicate any of this work, but to share various scientific understandings I have gleamed from numerous sources that confirm the deep inner knowingness that is a part of our innermost being. Most importantly, my purpose is to make clear the profound spiritual implications this knowledge can have on human consciousness and the future of the planet. As such, I apologise for any inaccuracies or inadvertent plagiarism!'

GOD IS SLOW!

Tuesday 30 September 2014

So at the time when I remember that I am God, and choose to embody Godliness, what do I do? I breathe deeply, I aim to channel and radiate peace and love, and I become very SLOW. Not in a sloth-like dumbed-down sort of way, but in a patient, attentive, deliberate and focussed sort of way. Life slows down around me, everything becomes easy and perfect, the present moment becomes paramount and life is good. Of course, the present is as slow as it gets – the present is eternal. God is slow. Go slowly, go with God.

NOT DOING IS A GREAT FREEDOM

Tuesday 30 September 2014

Too many things to do, not enough time to do them. Always caught in a state of wishing I could be...

One of the greatest freedoms I have found is in not doing – deliberately choosing NOT to do something – to cross things off the to-do list. When I decide not to check the emails I think I *should* be checking, I rule that anxiety out of my life. When I decide I'm not going to read that book I would like to read right now, I become free to enjoy what I *am* doing right now – which is generally being at peace (except for the thought about wanting to read that book). With that thought gone peace remains. When I attempt to meditate, to spend time with the kids or my wife, or to just relax, and when my mind starts telling me all the things I *should* be doing instead, I simply remind myself that the only thing I should / need / want to do is to be peace. I then choose to do nothing but be peace, the weight of *should* drops immediately of my shoulders and what I *am* doing right now becomes awesome.

ENLIGHTENMENT COMES AND GOES

Tuesday 30 September 2014

So is enlightenment an experience that once attained cannot be undone, or is it something that comes and goes? Is there a switch that is flicked on at some point that can't be turned off, or does the light flick on and off from time to time? I guess only those great individuals throughout history who seem to have maintained enlightenment indefinitely can answer – hopefully I can ask one of them some day. But until then, what I have come to understand about the concept of enlightenment tells me that is a state, and not a trait. We talk about 'God moments', 'Aha moments', 'thin places', times when everything is perfect, when we know exactly what to do and how to live, when we are fully immersed in the present and 'the light of consciousness shines through us' – times that unfortunately fade away. Are these moments of enlightenment? If so, the goal of enlightenment then is not simply to reach that state (most, if not all of us have had them), but to have them more and more regularly.

TREAT THEM LIKE PEOPLE

Wednesday 1 October 2014

"What I am saying is this - trust children!" John Holt

Brilliant advice. As I try harder and harder to get out of my kids' way (to stop interfering / dominating etc.), I find that every time I resist the urge to tell them what to / not to do, correct mistakes, or simply offer suggestions for improvements, I realise straight away just how restricting and disempowering, and especially how creativity-killing it would have been to do so. Ruby wrote a 6 chapter story all by herself yesterday (she is 6) and I wanted to correct her spelling or offer suggestions for this or that – thank God I didn't – it would have stripped her of the esteem she had in writing the story and removed her ownership over the whole thing.

Too often, I do the opposite – too often we treat kids like possessions or inferiors. Kids are people, we need to treat them like people – to trust them, to respect them, to speak to them as we would speak to a friend, a colleague or a neighbour. They are kids – we need to speak to them *more* respectfully and lovingly than we would another adult!

DON'T HIT IT – KISS IT!

Wednesday 1 October 2014

I've found myself having a short temper a little too frequently again lately and decided I need to re-implement one of the best changes in behaviour I have ever put into place. Six years ago I read "The 7 habits of highly effective teens" and among many other great insights, learnt that to break a bad habit we can't just drop it – we have to *replace* it. And to make a new habit, we have to do it religiously for a month.

So I gave it a crack. I realised that by far my worst habit was losing my cool over really small things. So I decided that I would replace an act of anger with an act of love, and each time I dropped something, or stubbed my toe, or heard a loud bang, instead of swearing, yelling, hitting or throwing something, I would kiss it! It sounds stupid, and every time I did it I *felt* stupid, and I immediately laughed and the anger dropped away – leaving me to realise the act of anger was the thing that was stupid in the first place!

We can't stop an emotion, but we can determine how long it lasts by taking powerful action. After less than a month, I didn't even really have to kiss too many things anymore as I wasn't getting angry about silly little things anymore. From time to time the bad habit starts creeping back in though and the odd kiss needs to come back out. If it's something you can't physically kiss, kiss it in your head instead (just picture yourself kissing your boss and your anger is bound to give way to humour!).

I'M BETTER WHEN I PRAY

Friday 3 October 2014

For most of my life I prayed every morning and every night. In recent years however, with changing beliefs and practices, I've fallen out of the habit, praying much less often. To get myself in the right frame of mind for each day, I have instead done various practices, from yoga to meditation, to inspirational readings, to visualisation and goal setting. These are all effective, and sometimes more so than at other times.

I've just realised lately however, that saying basically the same prayer I said every morning of my life is just as effective as any of these other practices. I always start with gratitude, listing off as many things as I can think of so say thank you for. And as countless studies now reveal, this is one of the best spiritual or well-being practices you can do. I then pray for certain people, and for all the things I would like to be (rather than have) – 'help me to love everyone and make everyone else happy', 'help me to be peaceful, patient, to be present etc. etc.', and because of this, I immediately *am* those things – much more than on days I don't do it.

My prayer is basically a combination of visualisation, goal setting, and meditation, but with added gratitude and compassion for others thrown into the mix (I wonder if I can start doing it during yoga??).

Why did I ever stop? I suppose I've had to make the leap from praying to an external being up in the clouds (in a way rejecting this God) to speaking directly to the divinity that I am (and coming home to this new image of God), and that took some time. It's a realisation that prayer was never about appeasing someone, or asking that someone to do or to give things to me, but about calling forth and letting God (the eternal goodness that is within me) shine through me.

Likewise with going to mass – while I rarely go anymore, and I cringe at much of what is said, I always feel better for having been. And this is simply for the fact that I have prayed (and been immersed in the love of what is being preached and of the community gathered) for an hour.

Time to get back into some old habits.

SEEDS OF WAR ARE IN US ALL.
WHICH ONE WILL YOU FEED?

Sunday 2 October 2014

Yesterday I went to my first ever Quakers meeting (on World Quaker Day) – basically an hour of silent meditation with a few people standing to make comment or read something. As Australia is just about to start air strikes on Iraq most of the comments centred around peace.

One comment was quite powerful – basically we all have to struggle against the seeds of war (the little bit of warmonger that is in us all), and it is the growth of these seeds that fills our homes, our towns, our cities, and then eventually our countries, that leads to full scale war – similar to the fantastic wisdom of Lao Tzu who said 2500 years ago:

> If there is to be peace in the world,
> There must be peace in the nations.
> If there is to be peace in the nations,
> There must be peace in the cities.
> If there is to be peace in the cities,
> There must be peace between neighbours.
> If there is to be peace between neighbours,
> There must be peace in the home.
> If there is to be peace in the home,
> There must be peace in the heart.

It is this search for peace in my heart that is the most important thing I can do to make world peace, but it is a goal that requires constant attention. As the Cherokee elder said to his grandson "there are two wolves fighting inside me – one is anger and violence, and the other is peace and love", and when the grandson asked which would win, the old man said "the one that I feed".

11

This morning the angry wolf won. As I slept next to Charlie, he for some reason started scratching my arm. In my dazed state I had a flash of anger at being woken and hurt and lashed out at his hands, only to miss and get his legs instead. The tears of my sleeping four-year-old gave me an instant reminder how tragically I have missed the mark again.

For centuries the angry wolf has grown fat and does not need much feeding to continue stomping on top of my peaceful wolf, who, though stronger, more powerful and intelligent, is also more hungry and needs a constant supply of goodness. This is my challenge. Luckily, I just started reading something really nutritious and Good Wolf is licking his lips! More on that soon.

TO HAVE FUN OF COURSE
Friday 10 October

So I'm torn between wanting to give kids complete free reign and providing some structure to motivate and keep them on track. And then I'm thinking of all the criteria they have to be able to meet if I give structure, and I think to myself that the most important criterion is to be able to answer the question 'why are you doing this?' 'What is your purpose?' And then it hits me – this is why free range is the way to go – because kids have actually got it right – they generally have one purpose and one purpose only – the most important purpose there is. If you give a kid the opportunity to literally do whatever they like, and then ask them what their purpose is in what they choose to do their answer will almost always be 'to have fun – der!!'

Isn't this the message we want kids to hear all the time – you don't need to have / do / accumulate things to be happy in the future, you can be happy with what you have right here right now. You can enjoy the fullness of life by immersing yourself in the wonder and awesomeness of the present moment. But then I want them to tell me they are working on some project so that they can achieve something in the future! No! I want you to do something because you love doing it – because it feels right and it feels good – because it is fun and because it makes you happy. My only guidance then needs to be to ensure that what they are doing will actually produce lasting happiness (by enhancing your own and other people's well-being) rather than momentary highs.

You don't have to write a book because you want to make people happy or influence them. You write a book because you love writing, and then your book is bound to make others happy.

Hmmm, very fresh insight – think it sounds valid – will give it some more thought.

ALL YOU HAVE TO DO IS FLICK THE SWITCH
Thursday 6 November 2014

Nurturing your spiritual, emotional, mental, and physical well-being is as simple as this. At all moments in life, your body is continually releasing either hormones that are damaging to the body and mind (adrenaline, cortisol etc.), or hormones that heal the body and mind (serotonin, oxytocin etc.). Your body can't release them both at the same time – it is one or another. And it is this simple: when you are in a state of flight or fright you release damaging hormones, when you are not, you release the healing ones.

So we are releasing the good hormones most of the time right? Wrong! The thing is that the flight or fight response has many degrees – from big, sudden scares, to minor, even subconscious stresses. The fact is that most of us are in a state of flight or fight most of the time – from major fear or anger, to nagging stress and anxiety. Feel your forehead right now, or your jaw, shoulders or back. Chances are you can feel this nagging tightness even during times of seeming calm. In our modern world, we tend to be constantly on edge – constantly on the look out to protect ourselves, with occasional (or sometimes regular) flare ups of these emotions – and therefore constantly flooding every cell in our bodies with chemicals that break down tissue, cause sickness and aging, and degrade our emotional well-being.

The good news, is that when we switch off the flight or fight response (and therefore these damaging hormones) we automatically switch on the relaxation response, which floods every cell in our bodies with chemicals that heal, rejuvenate and relax our bodies and enhance our emotional wellbeing. The only question then is how to flick this switch. That too is very easy – you just have to remember to do it, and do it often.

ANSWER EVERY QUESTION

Thursday 13 November 2014

As a teacher, I now realise that the main thing I want is for people to ask me questions. The other day I was watching the all-time classic "The Shawshank Redemption" with Will, and he did the usual kid thing of asking a million questions about the move right throughout it, and I did the dad thing of getting annoyed that he was making me miss what was being said and giving short, frustrated answers.

Then it finally hit me (thank God): "You idiot! (in a nice way). This is exactly what you want him to be doing! You want your seven year old son to be asking lots of questions. This is a golden moment to learn about life – to 'unschool'. How many precious learning opportunities had I missed in the past by ignoring his questions? More importantly, how many times had I crushed his curiosity, cut off his reaching out to connect to me, and squashed his self-worth by telling him "just be quiet and watch"? What a terrible, terrible thing to say.

I used to do it in class too – "sorry, we're not talking about that now – let's get back on track with me explaining something else (that is clearly boring you)". I'm now coming to realise that what a teacher really wants is for students to ask questions. We try to spark curiosity, we try to manufacture engagement, we try to make them listen to us, when what we really want, what true teaching is all about, is being there to answer the questions they ask us – and they'll stop doing that pretty quick if we just keep doing it our way instead.

Anyone who has had a toddler will know how many million questions they ask every day, and every one of us has found this incredibly frustrating at least at times. But this is how they learn! This is what we could crave and thrive on as a parent. It's not easy to put what we are doing aside to give our attention, but the best thing we can ever do for our kids learning is to answer every questions! With love!

Thank God this realisation came to me after just the second or third question. We went on to discuss throughout the movie all sorts of things from taxes, to fraud, to gun laws, suicide, and freedom. I ended up letting Will stay up till 11.30 with me to watch the whole thing (how could you not let him see Andy standing in the sewer in the rain a free man!) and it was the best spent three hours I've had in a long time.

WORKING ON THE SHADOW

Sunday 23 November 2014

This weekend I had about 12 hours of good old fashioned non-presence and losing my cool. Here are some insights:

- I knew it was happening, but either couldn't get out of it, or didn't think I needed to. I allowed it to gradually build up to the point where I got triggered to really lose it.

- I hadn't really practiced mindfulness for a few days before hand – again slipping into thinking I don't need to – but clearly I do. What happens is the awareness of Oneness slowly disappears, the illusion of separateness slowly builds, and things gradually seem to matter when they really don't.

- I realised how rare this has become – that I really have been peaceful the vast majority of the time, and even when I dip a bit I generally act effectively despite my mental state.

- I realised it really is in the subconscious that suffering / stress / anxiety happens. When I slip into this state, positive self-talk in the conscious mind doesn't override the background disease in the subconscious. What does work in this state is to simply be aware of this, and to become REALLY present. It's like when I am in the zone the conscious mind is positive and the subconscious either quiet or positive too. When not in the zone, the ego goes underground (into the subconscious) and this is when being really mindful in

17

the present is really effective.

- I really came to see how "the shadow" works. What triggered me (really made me mad) was Charlie being violent. Because it is so important for me not to be violent, the violent part of me reacted really strongly when someone else is violent. Again, the key to this is awareness. Will keep working on it.

As they say, every experience is important for our learning and growth. Hopefully I learn the above from this and it becomes more and more rare still.

BEING HOPE-FILLED – EMBRACE MYSTERY

Friday 3 December 2014

The wolves are the two different responses!

Every person has a constant battle going on within them between the stress response (release of physically damaging hormones as a result of flight or fight reaction), and the relaxation response (release of healing hormones when flight or flight is switched off). This battle is the physical reality of the Native American story of the elder who described the two wolves who were fighting within him (one peaceful and one violent).

This is what personal wellness comes down to – how often the peaceful wolf (the relaxation response) is winning the battle. The elder tells us the wolf that will win is the one he feeds. So how do we feed them? We feed them with our minds. And how do we feed the peaceful wolf? We feed it with HOPE And now I finally get what that word means.

In Lissa Rankin's book, *Mind Over Medicine,* she describes how the relaxation response triggers the placebo effect and spontaneous remission from disease when patients genuinely believe they will get well, and in a broader sense, how the relaxation response switches on the body's self-healing mechanisms when people believe that things are good. In other words, what feeds our peaceful wolf, what relaxes our body, floods each cell in it with feel-good hormones that heal the body is HOPE. But when you think of what is actually happening in the process, the word hope takes on a much more specific and powerful meaning than we previously ascribed to it.

Hope is about more than just positivity and optimism – it is about being open to, embracing, and then delving deeply into, the realms of wonderment, awe, mystery, the unbelievable, the unimaginable, the impossible. This is the mother-load of flicking on the relaxation response and healing the mind and body! We need to be amazed! We need to believe! In all sorts of things. This is what religious belief in God / heaven / life after death etc. have always given people. But it is what is also provided when we stare into and explore the unimaginable vastness and connection of the universe, when we are fully immersed in nature, when we are fully immersed in the present moment, when we become aware of the unfathomable beauty and perfection in another human being, when we experience beauty and love pouring through all forms of art, when we discover all sorts of new scientific, spiritual and philosophical discoveries and insights and hear all sorts of amazing stories, when we care for others and believe in our power to change the world. It's what writing this does to me now, and hopefully to you reading it now.

"Being hope-filled people" is a central concept within Christianity, but being hope-filled is about more than just positive thinking and having certain conscious beliefs. The fact is that despite our conscious thoughts and beliefs, more than 95% of the time our bodies are run by our subconscious mind. And through our conditioning, most of this subconscious activity feeds our violent wolf, turning on our stress response. Genuine, radical hope is about an experience of deep mystery, and this cuts through our subconscious mind. It is being a dreamer, a mystic, what some would call a gullible fool or a hippy. The fact is though, that whatever mystery, belief or wonder that you allow yourself to dive into – whether it turns out to be true or not – it feeds your peaceful wolf. It is the ticket to living peacefully, positively and joyfully at both the conscious and subconscious level, and switching on all of the *extraordinary* self-repair mechanisms your body knows how to run on a physiological level (if you believe in that of course!).

NOTHING MATTERS BUT
EVERYTHING MATTERS

Wednesday 24 December 2014

This is the great paradox. Ultimately, in the big (cosmic) scheme of things, we (and everything to do with us) is so insignificant, so inconsequential, so, so minute and so, so fleeting. In the big scheme of things we are much less than a speck of dust, less than a blip in time. We are like ants - here today, gone tomorrow – both as individuals and as a species. Our world, our sun, and even our galaxy exist for the briefest of moments in the history of an unfathomably immense cosmos. This is our ultimate source of peace – it is our beautiful, perfect, eternal reality when our individual bodies die, and it is our permission to let go, to surrender to the isness, the nowness, the perfection, of our earthly lives.

And yet, the moment of realisation that nothing matters is the immediate realisation that, at the same time, everything matters. Our fleetingness demands our attention to live life most fully – to seize every moment – to leave our mark and make our tiny blip count. Our utter connection with all that is demands our concern and care for all of life – to end suffering – to bring peace to all creatures and to the earth itself'. And our peaceful, joyous surrender to what is empowers us with infinite wisdom and strength to fulfil both of these demands. The trick is to fully realise it.

NOT LIVING IN THE LAND OF TEMPERS

Thursday 25 December 2014

I've just returned from a few more days in "The Land of Tempers".

A few days ago I was reading to Ruby Enid Blyton's *The Far Away Tree* in which a group of kids go on a series of adventures to different lands that appear at the top of an enchanted tree (the land of presents, the land of do as you please, the land of dreams etc.). One such land was the "Land of Tempers" – a place where everyone is angry, yelling, carrying on etc. The deal was that if you visit the Land of Tempers and lose your temper you get stuck there forever. What a metaphor for life! When the children arrived in the land they were confronted by a series of rude, angry people and they each began to get angry in return, until one of their friends said "quick, smile". They did, stayed calm, and when they had done what they needed to do left the land for good.

This is exactly what happens to me. I'll be "in the now" / "living in alignment" / whatever you want to call it, for a few days, and then I'll allow myself to get frustrated with something – I know at the time I shouldn't, but I think to myself "oh it's just this one thing – I can just let off some steam", or "this time I really *should* get frustrated / angry". And then it happens again not long after, and it only takes one or two more times and I have not just slipped back into old bad habits, but I have slipped out of the now – I am trapped in the Land of Tempers!! And in this land, even though I know what is happening I can't get out – I can't find the now again, until some sort of moment's grace, or until some practice snaps me back into it at some stage – usually several days later. At least unlike the book I'm not trapped forever.

So now I'm back, my aim is to say "quick, smile – kiss it" and not allow the temper to sneak back in. This isn't repression – repression only happens when I'm not in the now - that's why smiling / kissing in the Land of Tempers is far less effective. Now it is all good though.

YEAR TWO – DISCIPLINE NEEDED

Friday 16 January 2015

Welcome to 2015 (a couple of weeks late!). My beautiful little sister bought me a mindfulness journal for Christmas and I wrote this about a week ago in it as I start my *second year of living peacefully*:

Year one went really well with moments of not-as-peaceful-as-requested. What I've found in these last couple of unstructured weeks of holiday is that my mindful practice needs to be more disciplined, so here are my 2015 New Year's Resolutions to being mindful and peaceful:

1. Meditate at least 5 - 20 minutes every day (I'm going to aim for midday, but morning or night will do too)

2. Start every day peacefully – (breath / body – live in the moment before work, meditate, read, yoga, pray – gratitude and reminders)

3. Set daily reminders / bells (driving / toilet, talking to people – STRICT). Hopefully new fitbit and focus band soon to help

4. Kiss more stuff!

5. Use the 12 pathways to higher consciousness constantly

6. Be God!!

7. See others' needs rather than words / actions (Aldort – read every second day at least)

8. Think win-win!

My one (three) little words for the year:
- Adandon (from last year – too good to stop)
- Release
- Flow

Happy 2015

THIS IS WHAT I'M DOING AND BULL SHOULD!!

Monday 19 January 2015

Another mantra I haven't used for a while but so powerful.

Whenever you're feeling bored / anxious / aimless just ask "what are you going to do right now?" then do it! And shout joyfully "THIS IS WHAT I AM DOING!". Therefore I "should" be doing something else is just "bullshould!" I should NOT be doing something else because I am NOT!

All you have to do then is powerfully choose what you are going to do in each moment:

God, grant me the serenity to accept the things I cannot change (what I am doing now),
the courage to change the things I can (to do something else if I choose to)
and the wisdom to know the difference (to do what you really want to do).

And sometimes I like to reverse the serenity prayer:

God, grant me the wisdom to know the right thing to do,
the courage to change the things I can,
and the serenity to accept the things I can't.

WHOSE BUSINESS ARE YOU IN?

Sunday 15 February 2015

This is a short and simple one. Byron Katie tells us you can be in three different people's business: your business, my business, and God's business. If you are in my business (worrying about / trying to change me etc.), or in God's business (worrying about / trying to change things completely out of your control), you are going to suffer. You can still suffer if you are in your own business, but you are the only person you can control and change, so stay in your business.

You can still care for, and help other people and other situations, but doing so without stress or anxiety is how you do it effectively. Same with yourself!

WHAT TIME? WHOSE BUSINESS?
WHICH ADDICTION?

Friday 6 March 2015

Any time I suffer I can investigate it's source by asking myself the three key questions:

1. Am I living in the past, present, or future?

2. Who's business am I in (theirs, God's, or mine)?

3. Which addiction am I being drawn to (security, sensation, or power)?

If I am suffering, I am most likely regretting the past, or worrying about the future (which is pointless).

If I am suffering, I am most likely trying to solve the problems of the world or other people in my head (which makes them bigger!!!!). Loving surrender and empowered action makes them better.

If I am suffering, I am most likely being controlled by a conditioned need to seek some sort of security (which I always have really), some form of sensation (which I don't need) or some form of power over others (which is just crazy).

In finding the source of my suffering, I can curiously accept it, see its involuntary nature, and it's unnecessariness, and, peacefully and loving watch it disappear.

Then I am free of my addictions, I focus on my own business, and I live in the present moment. All is well!

IT REALLY IS ME!

Friday 6 March 2015

I've taken the next leap of faith in understanding our Oneness, my own shadow and ego, and how to heal the world.

So understanding we are all literally one, understanding I react to that in others that I have suppressed in myself, I now take really seriously the belief that the whole universe literally resides in me (not me in the universe). This means that EVERYTHING is happening in me. This means that everything I witness in the world is simply a projection of what is in me (and I am witnessing it from more than seven billion vantage points (+infinitely more)).

This means that when my shadow is triggered – i.e. when I witness something and react with fear, anger, anxiety etc., I am simply witnessing part of MYSELF that needs to be healed (not part of myself over there as another person, but part of myself IN HERE as me). It is part of me that has been suppressed or neglected (because I always blame or get angry at the other). It is projected onto "the other" because I cannot / do not want to see it in myself. It is crying out to me because it wants to be seen and to be healed.

So how is it healed? I really like what I have just read about the indigenous Hawaiian practice of ho'oponopono. Basically, I look inside myself for what part of me needs healing (is violent, scared, lonely etc – whatever you are witnessing in 'the other'). I see a neglected child within me reacting to an old bad memory, I tell the child I love it, I am sorry I have neglected and ignored it, I ask for its forgiveness, and I thank it. In doing this, I instantly forgive 'the other' and give absolute compassion and acceptance, I take ownership for my own thoughts and emotions, and I respond with love and peace.

I've only been at it for a couple of weeks but it has been fairly profound.

While not being triggered, ho'oponopono practice suggests the continual healing or 'cleaning' practice of repeating "I love you, I am sorry, please forgive me, thank you", which constantly heals the inner child / the shadow / the ego. Through visualisation, the child can do this itself even when you are not consciously doing it.

And, the beauty, love, peace, perfection I see in the world I now also see as a projection of the universe in me. The more I see it from my isolated vantage point, the more I see it from my seven billion other vantage points.

Namaste

ACCEPT FULL RESPONSIBILITY

Thursday 6 November 2014

Ho'oponopono, seeing myself in everything and everyone literally, has completely changed everything – massively! I'm not remembering to do it all the time, but a lot of the time, and it has made me realise the one spiritual teaching I've never fully got before – to accept complete responsibility for every single thing! But not in a judgemental way – there is absolutely nothing *wrong* with what I have manifested. The reality is that I haven't done anything *to* manifest what is – my subconscious has manifested what I *need* to experience and heal. So don't judge the other (there isn't one), don't judge me, just heal it. Just love.

Fully accepting everything means I no longer blame anyone, I am no longer angry at anyone, including myself. Awesome.

YOU'VE GOT TO LIVE IT

Wednesday 18 March 2015

Telling someone not to judge is great advice, someone might even agree with you, they might even try it somewhat, but they won't get it until they fully live and embrace it. It is only when you adopt a particular teaching as a way of life that you realise why. Forgiveness, not judging, serving others, giving, non-violence, – they are just good ideas until you live up to them. Then they become the most obvious things to do. You can't not do them.

I'M GETTING BETTER

Friday 20 March 2015

It's amazing how much my thoughts and language are continuing to evolve and improve of late. Really simple things, things I never realised were destructive. Like instead of saying "I'm going to be really strict about this" (which I thought was a more non-violent comment), saying "I am going to insist". Like instead of saying "you've had plenty of time to get this done, I don't see any reason why you wouldn't have finished by now", saying "I suspect you've probably been doing other things a fair bit of the time".

And it is in my thoughts now too. Hardly anything is ever a problem anymore – why would it be! I think back to things I used to think were normal and harmless. Like worrying about how someone might react (I still *care* how they might react but rarely *worry* now). Like waking up feeling stressed and anxious about work that day (that happened a little bit a couple of times last week and is was really unusual). I'm thinking peacefully *about* things – not just about *how* things are going to be. Don't get me wrong - there's still quite a few moments of forgetfulness, but peace is becoming less and less of a struggle / effort – it is becoming more and more a habit – more and more my default operating mode.

SEEING THINGS THROUGH THE "BIG" MIND

Friday 20 March 2015

So I've been seeing that we are all one, that there is one body, one mind, one soul etc. But I have been seeing with "my" mind. I've been applying it to "my" life – rather than seeing the "big mind" *through* the "big mind".

When you see Oneness through your own mind you see we are all connected, but that we are all having separate, individual journeys, and so we still can't make sense of it – we can't see why they suffer and I don't, or why they act / believe / do / have / are one thing and I act / have etc. differently. But when you see the big mind through the big mind, you see that we are all having THE SAME JOURNEY!!!!! It is not part of me, part of the big mind, that is suffering – it is the big mind suffering! It is not part of me that commits "evil" – it is the big mind that does it.

Separating "my" part of me from "your" part of me still creates judgement, blame, confusion, resentment, sorrow. The ocean can't blame the sea for being polluted – the whole ocean is polluted. My dad was asking me about Hitler, how could he be in heaven / not be evil etc. But this question can only be asked if you still think Hitler is somehow separate from you – in any way separate. Hitler is not part of you – Hitler IS YOU. Hitler's mind is *the* mind, Hitler's soul is *the* soul.

The best way I keep thinking of it is "I am experiencing the world through seven billion pairs of eyes (trillions more actually), but only aware of one of them right now". Just like every nerve cell in my body receives its one piece of information, and all 100 billion of them give me my picture of the world, my picture of the world is one of the 100 billion billion making up the picture of the "big" mind. Why do we still think orders of magnitude stop with us??

SOOTHE THEM WHILE YOU CAN

Friday 20 March 2015

A Year 5 boy was in tears yesterday because he missed out on his tuckshop day. I am so glad we were filled with compassion and got him something to eat, rather than telling him to toughen up. I'm so glad he felt loved, rather than judged and belittled. I'm so glad he was able to express his emotion – to let it out, rather than suppressing it – letting it build and grow inside. I'm so glad he was in Year 5, because a Year 9 boy wouldn't have cried – because he's been judged and belittled too many times before.

It made me realise – the opportunities I have to soothe my child's tears, to free them of their pain and cleanse it from their shadow / pain body / subconscious etc. become fewer and fewer as they get older and older. The older they get, the less love they receive, the more they repress, the more the pain builds. But the more I soothe now, the cleaner the shadow, the freer they become as adults.

HE WHO DIES WHEN HE DIES DOES NOT DIE WHEN HE DIES!

Friday 20 March 2015

When you realise you're not the little you, you realise the real you can never die. When you realise the real you can never die, the little you actually does die. Because the little you is now dead, when it really dies (in the flesh), *you* are already eternal.

SAYING SORRY IS HARD

Friday 20 March 2015

Saying sorry is hard – but it works. Even if you don't think you are wrong. Even if you think it will allow the other person to shift blame onto you. Do it anyway because the other person IS YOU!! You are saying sorry to yourself because YOU feel this way. Knowing this it is still really hard – it makes you realise how much resistance the ego really has – how much it holds on to being right even when you know "being right" makes things worse.

But you have to get this first, otherwise it won't work.

ABANDON!

Monday 30 March 2015

Watch Golden Buddha clip first:
https://www.youtube.com/watch?v=HCv7-x91G9k

Why do we find it so hard to find our own true nature? Life throws so much crap on to us – difficulties, traumas, criticism etc. etc. – they build up the masks / the outer casing of stone that obscures our true nature. But it even happens when things are going "ok" or even "well". We still wake up with the weight of a casing of subtle, nagging anxiety – which is all built from EXPECTATION – what we think we should do / be, or more specifically, what we think others think we should do / be.

We have to shake this off (Taylor Swift style!). My key word last year was ABANDON – take a deep breath, realise nothing really matters, and breathe off expectation / worry / masks / casing. You are perfect, what you do is perfect, what others do DOESN'T MATTER. Release / relax / abandon the casing and let the light shine through. Oh yeah...

I CAN LOVE

Wednesday 15 April 2015

Just had a 'Grace Attack' and thinking about what I am / could be an expert in. I'll never be an artist, I'll never be an expert teacher, preacher, writer, or guru. But I can love! I'm certainly no expert in this yet either. But love is a moment to moment experience. It's the one field where at any given moment, with inspiration or consciousness, I can be a Mozart, Van Gough, or Ponting. Doing it consistently takes practice, but doing it now is my birthright.

And this is the only field that matters!

YOU ARE GOOD ENOUGH

Saturday 18 April 2015

Today Em moved Charlie up on his rewards / helping chart from 7 to 8 (out of 12). He was so proud and excited. But then as he was looking up at that chart I heard his mind (subconsciously at least) say "I'm more than half good enough now" or "I'm nearly good enough now". Coinciding with reading *Parenting for a Peaceful World* by Robin Grille, who again condemns manipulative rewards, this was a terrible and profound realization. You are good enough right now little boy!

Luckily I saw this and said "put him straight to the top and leave him there" – where he belongs. We did and he didn't even want his reward. Time to once and for all scrap the reward ladder or just make a heap of them and put them straight to the top and leave them there. You are good enough little boy.

THEY LEARN FROM WHAT THEY SEE – I'M NOT LISTENING

Sunday 3 May 2015

Kid's don't learn behaviours from reward / punishment / consequences – they learn from what they see. In other words, kids don't grow up to do what we want them to do because they have been rewarded for doing it or punished for not doing it – they simply grow up to do what was done to them / in front of them.

So, saying "you will be quiet and listen to ME" actually teaches them NOT to listen because you are not! etc. etc. etc.

Today Charlie was arguing with me and then with Ruby (he wanted to go to golf and she didn't). He wasn't listening to me, and I was about to tell him to. He said, "dad I just want to tell you something", I was about to say, "no you will listen to me" when I caught myself and said, "ok I will listen to you Charlie". He said, "I don't want to go to golf because Ruby is sad." Imagine if I missed that thinking I was the boss.

Charlie has been doing a lot of "I'm not listening!" when we try to teach / correct him. My conditioned response is to get angry and want to say "you will listen to me." But the reality is this is his natural defence mechanism against our language which is actually damaging him. He is protecting himself from being made to feel there is something wrong with him and GOOD ON HIM. This means that when he grows up and he or others think or say negative things about him, his inner dialogue will say "I'm not listening" and that is a great thing! It is now my trigger to realise I need to speak to him in a way that he is happy to listen to.

I'M NOT NEARLY AS BUSY AS "I THINK" I AM – I AM PEACE!

Saturday 18 April 2015

The last couple of weeks I have been unusually stressed and anxious – feeling like I used to quite a bit of the time. Yes there is a fair bit happening or coming up, but I've been busier and much less stressed for a long time now. Then I realise that my mindful practice has been ordinary for the last couple of weeks. So yesterday I made sure I started the day with meditation, and practiced mindfulness properly throughout the day, and yes – that's what's been missing!

In the absence of my mindful practice, my mind has been wanting to think all the time – think of all the things I've got to do / want to do / am going to do / rehearsing things over and over. This is what I used to do, and it makes me realise that I'm not nearly as busy as my mind thinks I am. My mind thinks, and that makes me busy – all the time – in my mind!

The key that I have forgotten recently, is that when my mind tells me I 'should' be busy – 'should' be thinking or doing something - I just need to remind my mind that what I should be doing is being peace – that is my main and only real goal – I am peace, so BE peace!

TAKE YOUR GAME BRAIN OFF

Thursday 4 June 2015

When we've got something important to do we say we put our game face on. And it's good to do this when the game is on, but not all day every day. The truth is, most of the time, if we are not deliberately present, we are at work in our heads all the time. This is our gamebrain and we wear it way too much. It attaches itself the moment we wake up, and unchecked doesn't come off till we go back to bed. This is the state of mindlessness, which is usually stressful.

So, my new mantra is simply "take your gamebrain off". The key is to remember this first thing in the morning. Either do some formal meditation practice, or just refuse to think about work / what you have to do / enjoy the moment you are in. Doing it first thing in the morning makes it so much easier to do regularly throughout the day. The problem for so many people, and for me if I let it, is that the gamebrain attaches itself so fully that you forget what it is like not to have it on. You forget that you even have it. Wow it's good to take it off – especially 20 times a day. Doing it right now!

THE REAL PROBLEM WITH PRAISE. INTRINSIC MOTIVATION IS TAKING THINGS FOR GRANTED

Friday 26 June 2015

Yesterday we were at the park and Archie wanted to climb the big metal ladder to go on the slide. He wanted me to help him but I encouraged him to do it himself which he eventually did and then proceeded to climb it a dozen or so times all by himself.

My conditioned response was to want to lavish him with praise – "good climbing mate!", "very clever Archie!", "wow Archie, that's great climbing!" – or worse – "what a big boy you are Archie!" or something like that – but I stopped myself and just let him experience it for himself. And what I realised in that moment, is that if I had have lavished the praise, it would have made him think there was something special about being able to climb a ladder – that is was something beyond his normal range of abilities – that he was punching above his weight – which in effect is like saying to him "you shouldn't be able to do that", "you are special for being able to do that", and worse again "I didn't think you could do that". The result is, while he might feel good about being special and punching above his weight, he sees a boundary, he sees himself working at (or above) his upper limit of ability, and in praising him, I am actually showing my doubt in him which he then sees in himself.

On the contrary, when he did show some doubt in his ability at the start, and I simply, calmly and confidently said "no you can do it – up you go – that's it – good job", and left it at that, he took his ability to climb a ladder for granted. It is not at the upper reaches of his ability anymore, it is just another thing he can now do. He's not special, he's not punching above his weight, he's just normal, he doesn't think there is anything unnatural about what he has just done. And this is what true intrinsic motivation is about – it is not a feel good moment, it is taking your own skills and abilities for granted – having the self-confidence to know that you can do whatever it is you want to do – either easily, or with a bit of hard work. Having praise lavished on me strips this away. So when we do that, kids will either try to do it again to please us, which is extrinsic and unfulfilling, or worse, they will shy away from doing it again in our presence because subconsciously they know my praise and adoration is actually showing my doubt in them and limiting their potential.

So there is a fine line when the kids do something really good. I need to show them I knew they could do that without going over the top, but also giving attention when it is asked for and not letting them think I don't care.

MY VISIT TO PINE – BRING ON DEMOCRATIC SCHOOLING

Friday 26 June 2015

On Wednesday I spent the day at Pine Community School – a P-6 independent, democratic school, and absolutely loved it. Here are my observations:

1. Kids were hugging their teachers and sitting in their laps, teachers were hugging students to encourage them and make them feel better – even bigger kids. This is what we do with our own kids and should be able to do as teachers.

2. Students were not told "you are wrong", or "there is something wrong with you" (indirectly or directly) often, if ever. So many times, if I was the parent or the teacher I would have given correction or instruction that would have given this message, but the teachers there did not – they let the kids be themselves without any judgement, and it didn't make them any worse – it made them the same if not better!

3. As much as I loved it, I noticed how conditioned I still am, and all my conditioned assumptions and expectations kept coming through – "these kids are wasting time", "they should be more serious", "they should be learning", "they should be quiet and listen", "are they really learning – how will they do at maths etc"?

4, They ate when they wanted to, they had no shoes (even the teacher), they were generally happy, they were having fun, they were kind to each other. Teachers said they would definitely send their kids there – "I'm grateful they will have a childhood".

5. Despite my conditioned response I kept reminding myself "this is what I want my kids to be able to do".

I'm not sure I could do it as a teacher but as a parent yep!

SEE THEIR HUMANITY

Wednesday 1 July 2015

I was talking to a couple of mates the other day about all the terrible stuff that is going on in the world today with extremists and terrorism etc., and they seemed to think that shutting out migrants and building bigger walls and bigger guns to protect ourselves so to speak was the best way to deal with it. And then I thought – a bit too late unfortunately – about something that I think Martin Luther King Jr once said – something along the lines of the only way we will ever overcome an enemy is to see their humanity – that we see them as human beings trying to do the best that they know how to do in this world, that we see them as ourselves, and that we are filled with compassion for them, especially as, if they are wanting to hurt us, they must be damaged human beings. A quote on a church billboard the other day said "an enemy is someone who's story we haven't heard yet".

And so, the only way to overcome the extremism that exists in the world, the only way to gain peace, is for us to see the humanity of the fanatics, and those who are different from us, and for them to see ours. Quite simply, this will never be possible while we keep building bigger walls and bigger guns. Sure, we need to protect ourselves at times, but we also need to work to embrace, and talk to our enemies, as much as possible, to love them. This goes for every conflict with every other person. See their humanity, and your chances of overcoming the conflict are much much greater.

QUICK SALVE, CAPTAIN OF THE SHIP, IT'S NOT AN EMERGENCY

Monday 6 July 2015

Seems basic now, but I've just worked out a couple of really simple and effective parenting tips:

1. A shortened SALVE (Self talk, Attention, Listening, Validation, Explain – from Naomi Aldort's *Raising Our Children, Raising Ourselves*) and "Captaining of the Ship": Simply repeat to the child what they want / what they said (listening and validation) and then very calmly, non-judgementally, firmly, non-emotionally say what is going to happen / what you are going to do. Working really well with Charlie.

2. When strong emotions / panicking coming through "It doesn't matter, it's not an emergency. Now what are you going to do about it?"

STEP INTO THE 'OTHER' WORLD

Thursday 23 July 2015

Getting my morning practice right is the biggest key to a successful day. It has a number of important ingredients: meditation / mindfulness, gratitude, inspirational reading, maybe music, prayer. But repeating exactly the same thing each day becomes sterile and less effective, so I have to ad-lib a bit to try to get it right each day. And some are better than others. But basically what I am doing is stepping into the other world – the real world – "the more beautiful world our hearts now is possible" (Charles Einstein – just started reading – great). It is shaking off this world – my conditioning, societal pressures and expectations – and entering the mysterious, the magnificent, the extraordinary. 'External' inspiration is important for this to open the door and see the other world, and stillness to experience its truth. I think I got it right today.

Abandon, you are me, love and peace

WHEN YOU ARE IN THE NOW YOU REALIZE HOW FAR OUR OF THE NOW YOU USUALLY ARE

Sunday 16 August 2015

Often I think I am doing alright – that I'm close to being "in the now" but just a little stressy. But when I am *really* in the now I realize that at those times I'm actually miles away. Do more to really get there and then float.

FLOAT

Sunday 16 AUGUST 2015

Just float

BODY + MIND + ACCEPTANCE + LOVE = PEACE

Wednesday 16 September 2015

I've manage to draw myself out of the vortex of ego a few times lately and think I'm working out the right formula. Till now I've found either being in the now or being trapped in ego depends largely on grace, and both build their own momentum. Usually knowing I am trapped in the vortex of ego doesn't mean I can get out of it. But I think this is the ticket:

1. Accept my current state – it is ok to feel this way. It is liberating to allow this state of being

2. Attention to body – this is all I have to do right now. 10 conscious breaths

3. At the same time, Attention to mind – in a funky state, simply being aware of now does not remove the background dis-ease – the mind's relentless nagging compulsion to think and to worry. So just notice this. Just notice how powerful it is – how automatic (not you) it is. Be curious. Now switch back to body and repeat, and repeat

4. LOVE! Being in the now is meaningless without abundant love flowing through you. See yourself in others. I love you. I am sorry. Please forgive me. Thank you.

How's that?

DON'T LISTEN TO THE VOICES – JUST LOVE

& REHEARSE FOR THE WORST

Sunday 18 October 2015

Have slipped back into some old mental habits – letting the ego (judgement, complaining, blaming etc.) go a bit. Very simple – don't follow those voices. Don't listen to them. Realise what they are and just love the person you are thinking about. They are you!

Secondly, a really powerful practice I do sometimes and should do more often is to "rehearse for the worst". In other words, rather than imagining the fight / argument that you are going to have with someone (as we usually do), imagine yourself being the picture of peaceful acceptance and action in the face of the worst 'the other' can throw at you. This completely changes your state of mind regardless of whether the situation actually arises or not, and prepares you to act properly on the off chance that it does. Gold

THE SECRET TO ONENESS IS LOVE

Sunday 18 October 2015

Thinking about all the various practices that help us experience Oneness more. And simply, the one that is most important is love. It is what Buddha was all about, what Jesus was all about, what Gandhi was all about. Just really, really love. Be a lake of loving kindness to all. Remember it and everything else falls into place.

WHY ARE WE SO SELFISH?

Wednesday 18 November 2015

Quick not to a mate after a conversation last night about why are we selfish, and why do people think they can have anything they want:

I reckon Jesus said you *can* have whatever you want (if you have faith you can move mountains, your faith has made you well etc.) – lots of hippy new age stuff about abundance etc. to back this up. But, we became selfish because we forgot the rest of what Jesus said – that what *works* (not what is right or wrong) is to choose to have whatever is in the best interests of all people and not just ourselves. But in choosing what is best for everyone that *is* actually in our own best interests – it is building the Kingdom of God both in your own heart and in the whole world.

You could call it the Capitalist Manifesto! Consumerism with a conscience!

FAKE IT TILL YOU MAKE IT

Friday 4 December 2015

It's all about starting each day well. As I've already discussed, the same old formula does not work every day – you have to keep looking to find what gets you 'in the now' – meditation, music, reading, prayer, gratitude etc. etc.

But what I have found lately is that whether you get there or not, it can dissolve pretty quickly if you don't consciously carry it into the rest of the day. Basically you have to "fake it till you make it". Elevate yourself to a plane of Godliness, slowness, peacefulness, love. Be regal. Float above the ego. Pretend to be God. Do it for long enough and God will flow in and all of a sudden you have made it.

In other words, your morning practice cannot be 5 or 10 minutes – it has to be your first hour at least.

Yesterday I blew up at Will big time – it was horrible. Why? Because I have been content for a few days to just be "ok" – basically calm and peaceful most of the time, but letting the background disease and mental chatter hover far too much. Gradually I am cut off more and more from wholeness until something minor makes me snap. When you truly float, the background disease comes to the surface – you can detect it and let it go.

Today is a day of presence. Good luck buddy!

EXPERIENCING SUFFERING THROUGH COMPASSION

Tuesday 8 December 2015

We are here to experience the full spectrum of existence – black and white, up and down, in and out, hot and cold. You cannot have one without the other. Without hot you could not know what cold is. Without dark you could not know what light is. In choosing to experience life we need duality. So to experience the ultimate peace, joy and love that we are, we need also to experience suffering. But we do not need to suffer directly ourselves. I can learn the lesson through genuine compassion for others' suffering. Remember there is no 'other'. There is only You. Thus, when you feel another's suffering you are experiencing your own suffering. When you let the love that is your true nature flow through your being into that person, you have learned the lesson (this time) and so do not need to suffer 'yourself'.

Love love love love love!!!!!

ARE YOU DREAMING?

Sunday 20 March 2016

Your life is a dream. So is mine. In reality you are having seven billion dreams (infinitely more actually) all at the same time. Realising this is good news. If it is a bad dream you can realise it is only a dream. If it is a good dream, you can enjoy and revel in the journey before you start the next one.

Either way, you can wake up within this dream. I wake up through meditation – through stillness, through silence. When I meditate I become aware of the usual heaviness, the dis-ease, the worry, the anxiety, the littleness of my personal story – of my ego. I wake up to my Oneness with All That Is and see the illusion of my in individual story and individual self as a beautiful dream – a dream I can watch with curiosity or enjoyment.

But when I forget to meditate I get swept up in this story – in this dream – in my littleness. I forget it is a dream and get trapped in what can sometimes be a nightmare.

The trick is to wake up as often as you can. Nothing much happens during an individual meditation, but when it is regular my life becomes a lucid dream – I am still dreaming, but now I know I am dreaming. And knowing I am dreaming, I can create whatever dream I want to experience.

GIVE THEM WHAT THEY NEED

Thursday 7 April 2016

I only have trouble with the kids when I think I am too busy to stop what I am doing and actually give them the attention that they deserve and whatever it is that they need – when I bark an order and expect it to be done straight away, or when I dismiss their request for connection with me in some way, hoping it will go away.

Like stopping to sharpen the saw saves a heap of time in the long run, so too does stopping to listen, to give attention, and to give them what they need save a heap of time – and emotional upset.

But of course "giving them what they need" does not mean giving them what they have asked for every time. What they need might be a firm no, they might need to be in their own space for a moment, they might need something completely different from what they think they need. But most of all what they need is simply my attention. They need me to STOP. To take a sacred pause. To show them that they are important and their needs are important.

And it is only when I stop, and give them attention, that I can actually work out what it is that they really need. Remember to SALVE, and life is sweet!

BE DELIBERATE

Thursday 12 May 2016

Sometimes you get lucky – sometimes Grace happens. Sometimes you do spiritual practices incidentally or accidentally. And often you think this is good enough. It's not. It's good, but it's not enough. You have to deliberately practice – every morning, every day, every night. Be Deliberate!

THERE ARE NO PROBLEMS

Sunday 22 May 2016

I've fallen back into the trap of thinking I need to solve all of the problems of the world in my head all day long. But when I am still, when I am silent, when I really get into the present moment problems solve themselves. In fact, when present I realise there were never any problems in the first place.

IT HAS TO BE REGULAR – COUNT THE BREATHS

Monday 10 October 2016

It is times when you finally get back "in the now" after being out of it for a while that you realise how much the ego can grab hold of you, but as Alan Watts says in *The Handbook to Higher Consciousness* 'I welcome the opportunity (even if painful) that my minute-to-minute experience offers me to become aware of the addictions I must reprogram to be liberated from my robot-like emotional patterns" (Pathway 3) – it is these times that offer some real insight.

I've been really slack lately – hardly meditating at all, and significantly, not practicing regular mindfulness throughout the day. And what I have realised is that "you usually only shake it half off!" In other words, when you are really not present, and you realise it, and try and "shake it off," you only ever really get half-way there – you get a conscious awareness of what is going on and where you want to be, but it is not until you really get back into the habit of "being here now" regularly, that you really get here now! It is a reminder that regular meditation and mindfulness really is the key.

For the last few days I have been getting back into the habit, and particularly, remembering regularly throughout the day, to simply count 10 conscious breaths. And this has been the ticket. Today I have genuinely been back "in the now" for the first time in a while – and gee it feels good! I was starting to think I might be losing it – but it really was only a lack of practice. Glad I've got it back!

BE ALERT. DON'T THINK!

Thursday 13 October 2016

I've been listening to Eckhart Tolle again (should do it much more often), and been reminded that mindfulness is not just relaxation, calming, making yourself 'slow,' – it is about being alert! Being fully alive – making the senses more sensitive – being fully in the moment – not shutting stuff out, but soaking stuff up.

At the same time, it is about choosing not to think. I know people often say you're not supposed to try not to think, but I realise I need to remind myself more often not to allow thought to sweep me away – because it happens really quickly. I think I need to think but I really don't, and need to choose not to (or to just watch thoughts) much more often. Having a good week of reminders.

NIGHT MEDITATION IS MORE IMPORTANT THAN YOU THINK

Thursday 13 October 2016

While my days are definitely more peaceful when I meditate in the morning, and I've never really given a lot of value to night meditation, I am realising that some mornings you wake up feeling a bit 'stressy' and others you don't. So some are easy to get in the now, and others are not. And I reckon it is usually those nights that I get in the now before bed, that I wake up feeling so much better, and easier to get in the flow the next day. Need to do some more experimentation.

KEEP BEING HERE – NO PAST, NO FUTURE

Saturday 12 November 2016

Often I forget just how simply it really is. Just be here now. Rather than trying lots of different things and wondering why I'm not quite there, just remember EVERY time I feel uncomfortable it is because I am either in past or future. Just realise this and then allow yourself to come back here now, and again, and again, and again. You've got to keep doing it over and over before the train runs away.

LOVE, GRATITUDE, AND JOY

Thursday 22 December 2016

Have watched Christie-Maree Sheldon's talk on "Love or Above" again which says that everything is energy and we choose which energy we operate from every minute of every day. She says we want to operate from the energy of love or above. I want to operate at the energies of love, gratitude and joy.

Three really powerful energies which radiate out and heal the world.

So, I am reminding myself as often as I can to be: love (I love you, you are me) with everyone I meet; grateful (for everything I have right now), and joyful (have fun!)

These are lighter frequencies of energy so you just have to remember and let them shine. Be light!

REMEMBER GRATITUDE!!

Thursday 22 December 2016

I just wrote about love, gratitude and joy and realise the one that I forget to use the most often is gratitude.

It is so powerful and so easy, and yet I forget it so often. Remember as often as possible.Every minute of every day, you have so much to be grateful for. And in being grateful life feels awesome.

Even the difficult things – even the so-called 'bad' things – be grateful for them because they teach you, they help you, they guide you, they make you who you are today, and they make this life magnificent!

LOVE OR ABOVE

Sunday 1 January 2017

It took me four years, but today I finally published my book: *You Are Infinite, You Are Eternal, You Are God: And more importantly, You Are Me.* So yes, what started out as my one year of living peacefully (or attempting to) has ended up being three years, but I'm really glad it did, because this is what I have learned:

1. In the four years since I began writing the book, my assuredness that it is right has not wavered. My confidence as a writer certainly has at times, and some of the science has changed slightly, but the core message and underlying philosophy is rock solid – it can be no other way.

2. In terms of "being peaceful", or my goal of embodying the love and peace the book describes, I picture in my head a line graph. If love and peace is the vertical axis, and time the horizontal, I would say that the line has fluctuated up and down all over the place many times, but overall has trended upwards into a much better place. I have certainly not become an "enlightened master". I am certainly not the picture of blissful serenity and boundless compassion. I still sink into ego, frustration, anger, apathy far more often than I would like. I still see red with the kids from time to time. But on the whole, when I think back to the way I was 'most of the time' four years ago, I would say that I have definitely become a lot calmer, a lot more patient, a lot more understanding, less judgmental, and think

and speak in what I believe it a much more productive and effective manner.

3.   I am now far less self-conscious in terms of worrying about what people think of me as a person, a teacher, a leader, or about my wacky ideas. I have prioritized family, self-care, and "the things that really matter" far more over work, external stimulations, and trying to "save the world". As a result, I believe I have become a much better person, teacher, leader, husband and father, and have come to realise that "saving the world" is truly about "saving myself" first and foremost – it is about becoming the most peaceful, loving, contented, present me that I can be, and I am continuing to grow along this journey.

4.   And so that brings me to my final insight – to where I am now, and to my mission for 2017 and beyond, as I being my "fourth year of living peacefully'. For the last couple of weeks, my new mantra has been to be "Love or Above". I really like Christie-Marie Sheldon's description about the energy levels of each emotion and state of being. And I really like the idea of setting the intention that I consistently vibrate at the energy of love or above.

Each of the mantras I have used as the headings of these reflections posts over the past three years have been effective for short periods of time, and I end up cycling through them as I read over my reflections and remind myself of what works and what does not. But they all become a bit stale after a few days, and I need to move on to another. Over the past few weeks however, reminding myself regularly to be love or above – to be love, joy, and gratitude, has consistently dragged me into the present moment, into a positive, liberated state of mind, and to a reminder of my Oneness with others, with life, with God, with the universe itself, and it has stuck with me longer than any other mantra so far.

So this is my mission for 2017 and beyond. As I release my book today I commit from today onwards to be love or above. Christie tells us that a person vibrating consistently at the vibration of love can positively influence over 50 000 people. If my book can reach that many people, and have a positive influence on them all, I will feel extremely grateful. And if you end up reading this book, and it has had a positive influence on you as well, I am even more grateful still.

And then we continue the journey to vibrating higher and higher still and seeing what is really there!

Love and peace.

www.ingramcontent.com/pod-product-compliance
Lightning Source LLC
Chambersburg PA
CBHW021141020426
42331CB00005B/853